Dedication

This book is dedicated to all devotees of Lord Ganesha and followers of Sanatana Dharma

♡♡♡

KASHI'S FIFTY-SIX VINAYAKAS AND KING DIVODAS

SANTOSH KUMAR SINGH

Made with ♥ on the Notion Press Platform
www.notionpress.com

Contents

Contents

Contents

Prayer

Vakra-tunda, maha-kaya, surya-koti samaprabha, Nirvighnam kuru me deva, sarva-karyeshu sarvada.

ҏҏҏ

Ganga taranga ramaneya jata kalapam, Gauri nirantara vibhushita-vam bhagam. Narayana-priyamananga- madapaharam, Varanasi pura-patim bhaja-Vishwanatham.

ҏҏҏ

About The Author

Santosh Kumar Singh, born on June 15, 1964, hails from the culturally rich city of Varanasi. His father's name is Shri Shamsher Bahadur Singh.

Educational and Professional Experience:

With a strong foundation in primary education, Santosh obtained degrees in M.A., B.Ed., and B.P.Ed. His professional journey commenced with serving in the Indian Railways from 1990 to 2020. During these years, he held significant roles in various domains. Currently he is the National President of the World Vedic Sanatan Foundation, an important organization dedicated to promoting Vedic knowledge and Sanatan Dharma. Additionally, he has played pivotal roles as a guardian and Chief Executive Officer of the Garima Social Literature and Cultural Organization, emphasizing the importance of preserving and promoting Indian cultural heritage.

Literary and Artistic Endeavors:

Santosh Kumar Singh is not just a social worker but also an excellent author, filmmaker, and advocate for cultural revival. His literary contributions include the publication of books like "Shabd Suman," "Jindagi Ki Baatein," and "Kavya Garima," which compile unique collections of poems by 21 eminent poets. Furthermore, he has consistently produced films on social issues and cultural themes, contributing to social responsibility, awareness and cultural pride. His artistic endeavors have earned him recognition as a leading thinker in contemporary Indian cinema.

Perspective and Ideals:

At the core of Santosh's endeavors lies his life mantra, "Dharmo Rakshati Rakshitah," which means protecting Dharma ensures one's protection by Dharma. His life's resolve is to contribute to the establishment of a Sanatan nation in India and to reinstate Sanatan values. Through his unexpected efforts and initiatives, he has successfully left indelible marks on the hearts and minds of citizens, instilling a sense of social responsibility, awareness, and cultural pride.

In summary, Santosh Kumar Singh emerges as a beacon of hope and inspiration, truly a genuine cultural ambassador and social reformer dedicated to the upliftment of society and the preservation of Indian heritage.

Preface

I take immense pride in being born on this Earth, especially in the city of Mahadev, the sacred Kashi. With Mahadev's grace, I have never felt a lack of anything in life. As I approached the age of fifty, a desire awakened within me to re-establish the values of our eternal religion towards Kashi, and with this sentiment, I laid the foundation of the Vishwa Vedic Sanatan Trust.

I also decided to undertake a legal struggle to return the Gyanvapi Mosque, which was originally the Kashi Vishwanath Temple, back to the Hindus. Meanwhile, I engaged in discussions with some scholars about Kashi, during which I learned about the 56 Vinayaks of Kashi, which are an important part of Kashi's mythological history. This led me to commence an in-depth research on the subject.

Driven by curiosity to learn more about the prestige of these 56 Vinayaks, I discovered that most of these Vinayak statues have been damaged, some have been relocated, and some are now untraceable.

This distressing state deeply saddened me, and I resolved to re-establish them.

To understand the story behind the establishment of the 56 Vinayaks in Kashi, I studied various mythological texts, including the Skanda Purana. The story of King Divodas stood out to me as the most astonishing during my study. During my research, I encountered startling information that deeply impacted me. A student from London, Isabelle Bermijan, completed her PhD research on the 56 Vinayaks of Kashi between 1995 and 1999 while living in Kashi. Her PhD thesis provided me with many significant and in-depth insights, which were new and enlightening to me. During this research, I decided to write a book in both Hindi and

English, providing information about King Divodas and the 56 Vinayaks of Kashi.

In my resolve to revive most of the damaged and destroyed Vinayaks, I thought of commissioning paintings of all 56 Vinayaks by an artist connected with the Sanatan Dharma. For this significant task, I chose Dr. Neha Singh, a renowned international artist from the city, who had made her mark in the Guinness World Records by creating the largest painting of the Bhagavad Gita. She completed this exceptional task within about a year.

After completing all these tasks, I am moving forward to rejuvenate this wonderful mythology.

I humbly dedicate this book to the followers and lovers of Sanatan Dharma worldwide.

Santosh Kumar Singh
National President : Vishwa Vaidik Sanatana Nyas, Kashi

KING DIVODAS (RIPUNJAY)

Brief Introduction Of King Divodas

Divodas is a great mythological figure known as the king of Kashi. His original name was Ripunjaya. He pleased Lord Brahma with his penance, and as a result, he was given the name 'Divodas'. He expelled all the gods from Kashi and took over all their duties himself. He became renowned as a very skilled and duty-bound king.

Divodas was born in the lineage of Rajarshi Manu. He pleased Lord Brahma with his penance, after which Lord Brahma blessed him with divine powers to govern the Earth. Lord Brahma told him that he would give him the daughter of Nagraj Vasuki, Anangmohini, as his wife and that the gods would support his kingdom. Afterward, Ripunjaya requested Lord Brahma that the gods should stay in heaven and not come to Earth, so that humans could live happily without any obstacles. Lord Brahma accepted his prayer. Following this, King Divodas announced in his kingdom that gods and serpents would reside in heaven, and humans would live healthily and happily on Earth.

During Divodas's reign, Kashi was his capital. When he expelled all the gods from Kashi, Lord Brahma advised Lord Shiva to go to Mandarachal mountain. Lord Shiva performed penance on Mandarachal mountain and, as per Lord Brahma's words, started residing there. After Lord Shiva left, all the gods also moved to Mandarachal mountain. Lord Vishnu also abandoned the Vaishnava pilgrimage sites on Earth and went to Mandarachal mountain.

King Divodas established a strong capital in Kashi and ruled his subjects righteously. In his kingdom, even the serpent race did not commit any crimes. Demons served in human form. The Guhyakas acted as spies for the king among humans. No one defeated the scholars and ministers sitting in King Divodas's assembly in the scriptures, and his warriors were unbeaten in the battlefield. His kingdom was considered an ideal state.

The gods tried many times to find a fault in Divodas but were unsuccessful. Then, Lord Mahadev sent sixty-four Yoginis to Kashi to find any fault in the king. However, the Yoginis could not find any fault in Divodas either. They tried continuously in various forms in Kashi but could not find any fault in the king's conduct. Their efforts also did not succeed, and they eventually returned, expressing respect for the king's ideal governance and policies. Thus, the prestige of King Divodas's loyal governance towards his subjects became even more solidified. His kingdom maintained an atmosphere of righteousness, justice, and peace. This was evidence of Divodas's impeccable and ideal politics.

Lord Shiva had a special attachment to Kashi, so when even Suryadev did not return, Shiva sent Lord Brahma to Kashi. Lord Brahma disguised himself as an old Brahmin and met King Divodas, expressing his desire to perform a Yajna in Kashi, which the king facilitated. This Yajna site was later known as 'Dashashwamedh'. But Lord Brahma, not finding any fault in King Divodas, did not return. Then, Lord Ganesha came from Mandarachal to Kashi and became an astrologer in the guise of an old Brahmin. He impressed everyone with his divine vision and reached the king.

The king asked Lord Ganesha for guidance on his welfare, to which he replied that a Brahmin would come from the north on the eighteenth day to give advice. Lord Ganesha, not finding any fault in the king, did not return either. After that, Lord Vishnu was sent to Kashi. Vishnu, along with Garuda, arrived there, naming himself Punyakirti and Garuda as Vinayakirti. They resided in Dharmakshetra (Sarnath). On the eighteenth day, they reached the king, where the king himself admitted his pride in his penance.

Disclaimer

"The views expressed in this book are solely those of the author and do not reflect the opinions of any organization or individual. The author has made every effort to ensure the accuracy and completeness of the information provided in this book.

The author respects the right to freedom of speech and expression guaranteed by Article 19(1)(a) of the Constitution of India."

The Origin Of 56 Vinayakas And The Story Of King Divodas In Detail

King Divodas known initially as Ripunjay, is a narrative of devotion, duty, and divine favor. Ripunjay appeased the creator god Brahma through his penance. Brahma chose him as the guardian of the Earth and blessed him with immense divine powers and the hand of Anang Mohini, the daughter of the serpent king Vasuki, as his wife. The gods, satisfied with his governance, bestowed upon him heavenly gems and flowers. Following Brahma's blessing, he assumed the name Divodas from Ripunjay.

King Ripunjay humbly accepted Brahma's command and praised him in many ways. He inquired why, despite the presence of many other powerful and great kings, he was chosen for this role. Brahma responded that under the rule of a virtuous king like him, Indra would bring rain to the Earth, whereas under a sinful ruler, the gods would withhold it.

Ripunjay pleaded with Brahma for his reign to bring happiness and health to his subjects. Brahma affirmed this request with a "So be it." Subsequently, King Divodas announced in his kingdom that the gods would reside in heaven and serpents would not enter his domain, ensuring the health and happiness of humans. He also declared that during his rule, gods would stay in heaven, and humans on Earth would live happily and healthily. Thus, King Divodas laid the foundation for an ideal and blissful state for his subjects.

The description of King Divodas's righteous kingdom is both inspiring and exemplary. Sage Agastya asked Lord Shiva how he made King Divodas relinquish the city of Kashi. Kartikeya explained that Lord Shiva, pleased with the penance of King Mandar, moved to

Mandarachal mountain based on the words of Brahma. After Lord Shiva left, all the gods also moved to Mandarachal mountain. Lord Vishnu, too, abandoned the Vaishnava pilgrimages on Earth and went to Mandarachal, where Lord Shiva, the supreme deity, resided.

After the gods left the Earth, King Divodas ruled undisputedly. He established a governance system that was righteous and just, prioritizing the welfare and peace of his subjects above all. During his reign, his subjects were happy and prosperous, and there was a sense of brotherhood and goodwill among them. His kingdom was a paragon of dharma (righteousness), justice, and public welfare.

King Divodas, initially known as King Ripunjay, established a strong and prosperous capital in Kashi. His rule was marked by righteousness and care for his subjects, leading them on the path of progress. His power was considered greater than that of elephants, and even the residents of Naga-loka did not commit crimes in his kingdom. Demons took human form to serve him, and the Guhyakas acted as spies within his domain.

The scholars and ministers seated in King Divodas's assembly were so skilled that they were never defeated in debates. Similarly, his warriors were invincible in the battlefield and were never subdued by weapons. There was no one in his kingdom who was corrupted from their position or became the subject of others' hatred. Every person was stable and happy in their place.

All the villages in his kingdom were free from fear and worry. State officials were present in each village, ensuring the security and welfare of the people. Thus, his subjects were as wealthy and generous as Kubera, the god of wealth.

During his reign in Kashi, King Divodas spent eighty thousand years as if it were a single day. He nurtured his subjects like his own children, and never once did he gather even the slightest of sins.

His governance was based on justice, righteousness, and welfare, making Kashi an ideal and prosperous city.

King Divodas was knowledgeable in the six attributes of politics and was always enthusiastic due to his threefold powers. He was adept in strategy and deep in understanding, making it impossible for the gods to find any faults or weaknesses in him. In his kingdom, all men were monogamous, and all women were faithful to their husbands. Every Brahmin had studied the Vedas, every Kshatriya was valiant, every Vaishya was skilled in commerce, and the Shudras served the twice-born.

In his kingdom, celibates studied the Vedas in Gurukuls, and householders were skilled in hospitality and the knowledge of the Dharma Shastras. Those in the Vanaprastha stage lived in the forest, following the Vedic path. The Sannyasis were liberated in life, free from accumulation and desire. Even those born from Anuloma and Viloma practices followed their traditional dharma path.

In King Divodas's realm, there was no one childless, impoverished, neglectful of the elderly, or who died an untimely death. There were no fickle, talkative, deceitful, violent, hypocritical, jesters, orphans, and no one sold liquor. Everywhere there were discussions on scriptures and the chants of mantras. Everyone respected their elder brothers, masters, and husbands. All residents of Kashi engaged in the worship of deities, and scholars were honored upon receiving their desired objects.

In King Divodas's realm, there were plenty of righteous men who constructed wells, ponds, and gardens in abundance. People of all castes were content and fulfilled through excellent service works. The gods could not find any flaws or faults in his kingdom, making King Divodas's reign an example of an ideal, righteous, and blissful society.

According to Skanda, Indra and other gods introduced several obstacles to undermine King Divodas's governance. However, the virtuous King Divodas overcame all these challenges through his power of penance. Later, Lord Shiva sent 64 yoginis to Kashi to find any faults in King Divodas. Despite their continuous efforts for a year, they could not find any fault in the king and failed to influence him.

When the yoginis did not return, Lord Shiva sent Surya (the Sun God) to Kashi. He instructed Surya to expose any unrighteous acts by King Divodas in Kashi but not to disrespect him since insulting a virtuous person engaged in the path of dharma falls back as a great sin upon oneself. Surya was also commanded that if King Divodas deviated from dharma, he should desolate Kashi with his rays.

Surya Dev (Sun God) took various forms in Kashi, attempting different strategies. He appeared as a guest, beggar, philanthropist, impoverished person, astrologer, Brahmin, knower of the Brahman, Vedic scholar, Kshatriya, Vaishya, untouchable, celibate, householder, forest dweller, and ascetic. He tried to confuse people with different examples and narratives, teaching various vows, but in King Divodas's kingdom, he found nothing rare nor could he find any flaws. Thus, Surya Dev also failed in his efforts to find any fault in King Divodas's reign.

Skanda told Agastya that the virtuous King Divodas overcame all obstacles presented by the gods in Kashi through his power of penance. This demonstrates that whoever protects dharma in this transient body indeed protects all three worlds. Kashi is a rare and holy place, its importance surpassing all other wealth, property, and material things in the world. The brilliance of those residing in Kashi does not shine until their meritorious light is illuminated, keeping other glows ordinary.

Lord Surya resided in Kashi, expressing himself through his twelve forms. These include Lolarka, Uttararka, Sambaditya, Draupadaditya, Mayukhaditya, Khakholkaditya, Arunaditya, Vriddhaditya, Keshavaditya, Vimaladitya, Gangaditya, and Yamaditya. All these forms are located in Kashi, protecting the region. Lolarka, meaning the restless Sun desiring to see Kashi, became famous by this name. Located near Assi Sangam in the south, Lolarka fulfills the welfare of Kashi's residents. On the annual pilgrimage during the Margashirsha month's sixth or seventh day coinciding with Sunday, people are freed from all sins. Those who bathe at Assi Sangam, offer tarpan to gods and ancestors, and perform Shraddha rites as prescribed, are liberated from their ancestral debts. Viewing Lolarka and consuming its charanamrit (holy water) alleviates the sufferings of itch, eczema, and boils. Anyone who listens to the glory of Lolarka does not suffer in this world.

Skandaji tells Sage Agastya that when Surya Dev, also known as Anshumali, went to Kashi, Lord Shiva, residing on Mount Mandarachal, pondered that the yoginis and Surya Dev had not yet returned. He considered that Brahma Ji was capable of bringing news from Kashi. Therefore, he sent Brahma Ji to Kashi.

Upon reaching Kashi, Brahma Ji took the form of an old Brahmin, met King Divodas, and extended his hospitality. Brahma Ji praised the virtues of King Divodas, stating that he was a devout king whose qualities were rare among other kings. Brahma Ji requested King Divodas's assistance in performing a yajna.

King Divodas promised to help Brahma Ji, stating that his kingdom was dedicated to philanthropy. Brahma Ji then performed ten Ashwamedha Yajnas in Kashi, leading to the manifestation of the Dashashwamedh Ghat. In this holy place, all righteous acts like bathing, donating, chanting, fire sacrifices, studying scriptures, worshiping deities, evening prayers, offerings to ancestors, and performing Shraddha are eternally fruitful. Anyone who bathes in the Dashashwamedh Ghat and worships the Dashashwamedheshwar Lingam is liberated from all sins.

After the completion of King Divodas's yajna, Brahma Ji established a Brahmarshala there and resided in it. Thus, Brahma Ji also started living in Kashi. In this manner, Skandaji described the glory of Kashi and the devotion of King Divodas to dharma.

Skandaji further tells Sage Agastya about Lord Ganesha's journey to Kashi under the command of Lord Shiva. Ganesha left Mandarachal Mountain and arrived in Kashi, taking the form of a Brahmin. There, he assumed the guise of an old astrologer and visited each household, delighting the people. He entered the royal palace and, using his divine vision, accurately described objects, thereby gaining the trust of the women.

Queen Leelavati informed King Divodas about the Brahmin and advised him to meet him. The king summoned the Brahmin and accorded him due respect. Later, the king inquired about his future from the Brahmin, who told him that a Brahmin from the north would come on the eighteenth day to give him advice. Thus, Lord Ganesha took the entire city of Kashi under his influence.

Before King Divodas became the king of Kashi, Lord Ganesha adorned the places of his previous abode by assuming various forms. Following this, praises were sung for him, describing him as the conqueror of obstacles, the lord of all groups, a divine figure, the Vinayaka of Vedic hymns, and adorned with many virtues. Lord Ganesha's grace destroys all sins, and those who praise him become famous and prosperous. Men who worship Ganesha attain heaven and liberation. Those he looks upon have their sins destroyed, and such individuals can enter Kashi.

Skandji further tells Sage Agastya that when Lord Ganesha also delayed in Kashi, Lord Shiva requested Lord Vishnu to go to Kashi and urged him not to act as the ones sent before had done. Lord Vishnu said that whatever a man does, it is accomplished by contemplating the lotus feet of Lord Shiva. Then, after circumambulating Lord Shiva, he set out with Goddess Lakshmi from Mount Mandarachal and reached Kashi.

In Kashi, Lord Vishnu bathed at the confluence of the Ganga and Varuna rivers, which led to the creation of the 'Padodak' Tirtha. Bathing in this sacred spot erases the sins of seven lifetimes. Lord Vishnu himself crafted an idol from stone and worshipped it. Those who worship this idol attain Vaikuntha, the abode of Vishnu, and this place is known as 'Shvetadweep'. Subsequently, Lord Vishnu established his abode in 'Dharmakshetra' (Dharmachakra place - Sarnath), assuming the name Punyakirti, while Garuda took on the name Vinayakirti. Lord Vishnu imparted teachings of dharma to Garuda.

Thus, following the directive of Lord Shiva, Lord Ganesha and Lord Vishnu undertook their journey to Kashi and accomplished their respective tasks there.

Punyakirti, an incarnation of Lord Vishnu, provided King Divodas with teachings on dharma. He explained that after considering various scriptures, the sages have advocated for four types of charity: giving fearlessness to the frightened, medicine to the ill, education to students, and food to the hungry. Punyakirti also mentioned that liberation (moksha) occurs when ignorance (avidya) is eradicated, underscoring the Vedic principle that one should not harm any creature.

After these teachings, King Divodas established a Shivalinga and bid farewell to his kingdom's people. He anointed his son, Samarangaya, as king and constructed a temple near the Shivalinga, which became known as 'Bhoopalashree'. Afterwards, King Divodas was taken to the abode of Shiva in a divine chariot.

It is believed that those who read this story do not enter the womb again and all their desires are fulfilled. In this way, King Divodas ultimately attained liberation through adherence to his dharma and duties.

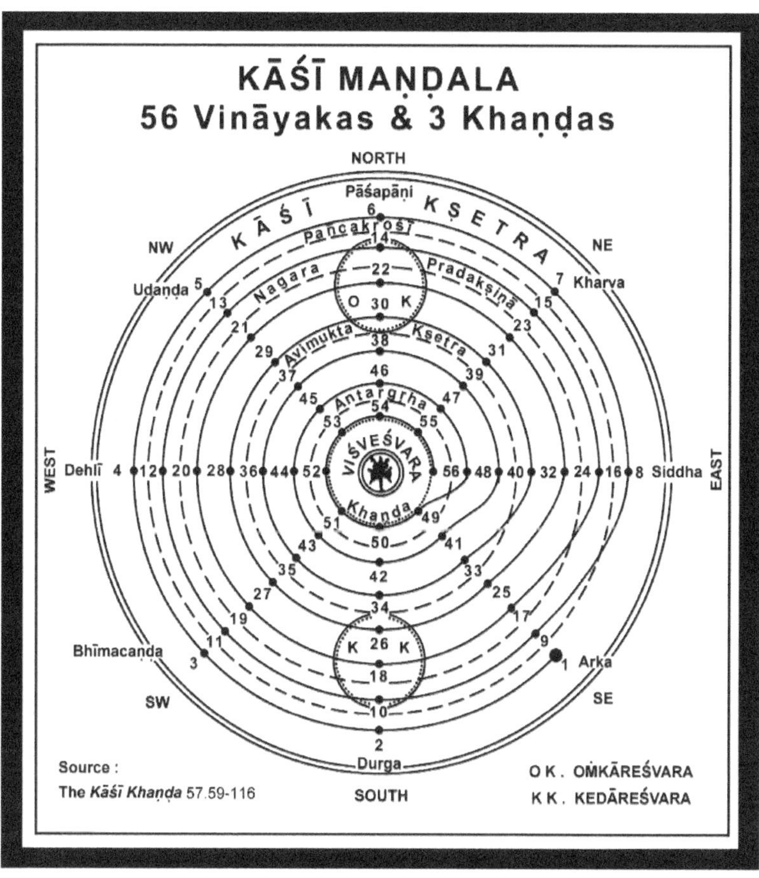

The ancient city of Varanasi has been designed in a unique way, like a divine painting or mandala. Lord Shiva resides in the middle of this sacred circle, established in the Vishwanath Temple and protected by concentric circles of divine guardians. To protect Kashi, fifty-six Vinayakas continue to guard Kashi by assuming seven forms in each of the eight directions.

THE FIRST FOLD OF EIGHT VINAYAKAS

ONE

SHRI ARK VINAYAK

Ark Vinayak (1-1), also known as 'Surya Vinayak', is located behind the Lolark Kund in Kashi, in front of the house at B 2/17. According to the Kashi Khand, this Vinayak is situated at the confluence of the Ganga and Assi in Kashi and is believed that viewing it on a Sunday alleviates all troubles. The role of Ark Vinayak is also associated with the worship of the sun at the Lolark Kund on Sundays. It is also mentioned in Tristhalisetu, Tirthaprakash, and Merutantra.

The main idol of this temple is approximately one and a half meters tall, and there is another idol of Ganesh close to it. This temple was constructed in the 18th century. The trunk of the idol is slightly turned towards the left, and one tooth is visible. The idol has four arms, with the upper right hand resting on the knee and possibly holding a rosary, while the upper left hand holds a lotus flower.

According to history, Ark Vinayak is one of those Vinayaks whose consecration date cannot be specified. It was an important temple during the Gahadavalas' time, likely the original Ark Vinayak was destroyed during Muslim invasions, and later a new idol was consecrated after restoration.

TWO

SHRI DURG VINAYAK

Durg Vinayak (2-1), located near the Durga temple in the southern part of the city, derives its name from its location. This Vinayak is situated in a separate temple near a pond, in the east direction of the Durga temple.

According to the Kashi Khand, this Vinayak, named Ganadhyaksha, is believed to eliminate all sorrows and should be worshiped with concentration. Although Kashi Khand does not describe it as located near Durga Devi, it is believed to have some connection with Durga Devi.

The idol of this Vinayak is about one and a half meters tall, and currently, most of its features are not clearly visible due to the clothes and floral garlands on it. The trunk of the idol hangs over the stomach, and Ganesh is shown sitting in a Lalitasana position. A silver crescent is adorned on the head.

Some pundits believe that the idols of Durga, Asha, and Siddhi Vinayak are copies of each other. However, there are notable differences between the idol of Asha Vinayak and Durg Vinayak, such as their height and the features of their faces and trunks.

The establishment of the Durg Vinayak idol is estimated to be in the

18th century, when Queen Bhavani had ordered the reconstruction of the pond and the restoration of the Durga temple.

THREE

Shri Bhimchand Vinayak

Bhimchanda Vinayak (3-1) gets its name from the term 'Bhimchandi,' a distorted form of 'Bhishmachandi,' meaning terrifying Chandi. This Vinayak, located in the precinct of the Bhimchandi Devi Temple during the Panchkroshi Yatra, is believed to eliminate all fears when visited, as per Kashi Khand.

It is also mentioned in Tristhalisetu and Tirthaprakash and categorized as 'Gneyashvanda Vinayak' in Merutantra.

The original idol of Bhimchanda Vinayak, excluding the mouse mount, is approximately sixty centimeters tall. The idol has a crown, characteristic of the third period, featuring a helmet-like structure and a top decoration on a petal-like base.

The trunk is turned to the left, touching a Modak container in the left hand. The upper right hand holds an axe, but the feature of the lower right hand is unclear. The lower left hand is holding a pot. Other ornaments of the idol are not clear, and the sacred thread is not visible on the idol.

According to locals, due to the top decoration on the crown, the idol appears to be from the 17th century rather than the 16th century. The function and position of this Vinayak are similar to that of the deity, suggesting some connection with the deity as well.

FOUR

SHRI DELHI VINAYAK

Delhi Vinayak is considered the protector of the western gate of Kashi, whose temple is located in Bhatouli village. The idol here is unique, depicting Vinayak standing on a mouse, with a simple crown and a third eye on the nose. The temple was constructed in the 18th century, and it is believed that the current idol might have replaced an older statue. The history of Delhi Vinayak is ancient, and a Ganesh idol found in the art museum of Kashi suggests its significance dating back to the 8th century. Outside the temple, there is a panel of sixteen Vinayaks, and it is visited during the Panchkroshi Yatra.

FIVE

Shri Uddanda Vinayak

The temple of Uddanda Vinayak (5-1), located near Rameshwar on the Panchkroshi Yatra route in the north-western part of Kashi, is famous for removing inappropriate obstacles for its devotees. The idol of this Vinayak is approximately 40-50 centimeters high, in a damaged condition, and it is holding a stick. There is no indication of a crown on the idol, and its trunk is turned to the left. Based on the roughness of the surface and the rigidity of the limbs, its construction is estimated to be between the fifteenth and sixteenth centuries. Unlike other idols, this Vinayak is not shown on a mouse, and there is no clear definition of its upper hands. One hand is on the stomach, possibly holding a rosary, while the lower left hand is damaged.

SIX

Shri Pashapani Vinayak

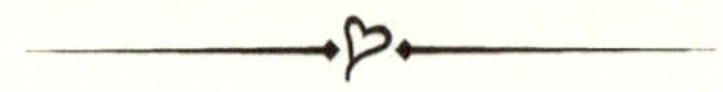

Pashapani Vinayak (6-1), known as the Vinayak holding a noose, has a temple located in the Sadar Bazaar in the north of Kashi. This location is part of both the Panchkroshi Yatra and the Nagar Pradakshina Yatra, which enhances its significance. There is a belief among the residents of Kashi that worshiping Pashapani Vinayak eradicates all obstacles. The idol is half a meter tall, in a Lalitasana posture with four hands, two of which are at the back and seem artificial, suggesting they might have been added later. One hand of the idol holds a noose, and another carries a lotus flower, while the lower hands hold a Modakapātra (sweet bowl) and a stick or mace. Its trunk and ears are also characteristic. Despite the idol being damaged, its features place it in the period between the thirteenth and fifteenth centuries. Outside the temple, there is another Ganesh idol which could be from the ninth or tenth century, raising questions about the origins of the idols and their original locations.

SEVEN

SHRI KHARV VINAYAK

Kharv Vinayak (7-1), referred to as 'Sundar Vinayak' in the Kashi Khand, is located on Adi Keshav Marg within the Rajghat Fort. This Vinayak is said to be situated at the confluence of the Ganges and Varuna rivers, where it removes the obstacles of devotees. The idol of Kharv Vinayak is about one meter tall, but due to damage to the base of the idol, it's difficult to clearly describe its posture. There is no crown or headband on its head, and its face appears elephant-like. It's presumed the idol has four arms, but the specific attributes are not clear. It wears a Nāg Yajnopavīta (sacred snake-thread), but details of other ornaments are missing. Its trunk is turned to the left and passes through a cut section.

A similar idol found in Kannauj, believed to be from the 7th century, helps in dating Kharv Vinayak. The better condition of the Kannauj idol assists in clearly identifying its attributes. The bare head, beautiful seated posture, and elephant-like face of Kharv Vinayak indicate its antiquity, although its damaged condition poses a challenge in classifying it accurately.

EIGHT

SHRI SIDDHI VINAYAK

Siddhi Vinayak (8-1), known as the protector of the eastern direction, is located near the Manikarnika Kund. The temple of Siddhi Vinayak is halfway up the stairs on the left side. According to the Kashi Khand, this Vinayak protects the holy site and bestows powers to the practitioners. The temple of Siddhi Vinayak is considered significant for visits at the beginning and end of pilgrimages. The idol is about one meter tall, adorned with a silver crown and has three large eyes, one of which has a shining lunar dot above the third eye. The trunk is turned to the left.

It is believed that the idol was established in the 19th century, and its installation could have been done by the Marathas or Peshwas. While there was mention of similarities between Durga, Siddhi, and Asha Vinayak, the characteristics of their trunks challenge this notion of similarity. The significance of Siddhi Vinayak and the tradition of their worship is widespread in India, making them exceptionally special and revered.

THE SECOND FOLD OF EIGHT VINAYAKAS

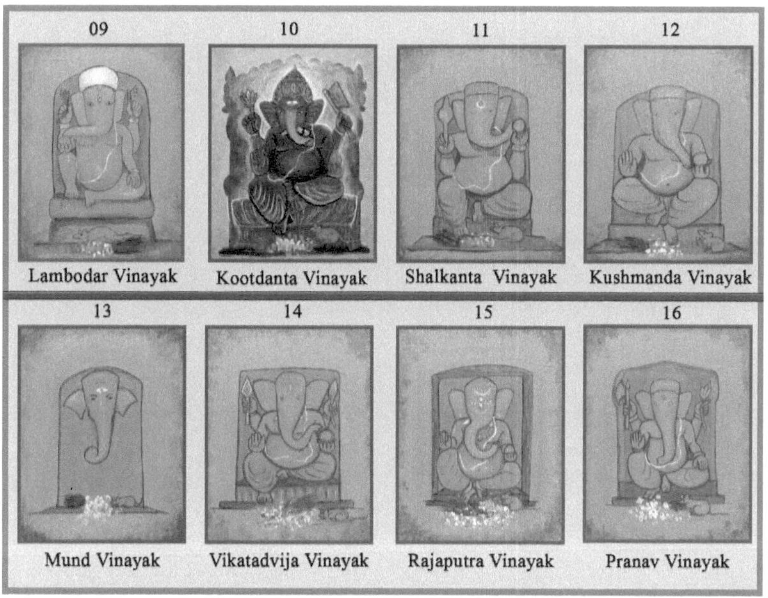

NINE

SHRI LAMBODAR VINAYAK

Lambodar Vinayak (9-2), also known as "Vinayak with the pot belly," is located in a small temple at the lower part of Lali Ghat, along the banks of the Ganga. This Vinayak is particularly visible from December to June, when the water level of the Ganga decreases. The current temple was built in recent years, and it houses an idol of Vinayak dancing, depicted with a mouse near his right foot.

The good condition of the idol and the presence of other statues with it suggest that it was originally established on the higher part of the ghat. Based on its dancing posture and the characteristics of its crown and the arms in the back, it can be assumed that Lambodar Vinayak might date back to the 13th or 14th century. The dancing form of this idol makes it unique and indicates its archaeological and religious significance.

TEN

SHRI KOOTDANT VINAYAK

Kootdant Vinayak (10-2), located at the Cream Kund in the Aghor compound in Ravindrapuri, is described in the Kashi Khand and also mentioned by Prinsep.

The idol depicts Vinayak seated with a crown on his head, the base of which is carved from a flower petal. His trunk is turned to the right and holds a modak, touching the right tusk. Vinayak is presented with two tusks, where the left tusk is shorter than the right.

This idol is an exemplary representation of Vinayaks from the nineteenth century, and its recent dating is confirmed by the statue and the ornaments on it. Interestingly, this idol is almost an exact replica of a Ganesh statue found in the Patna Museum, suggesting that the artist who carved Kootdant Vinayak may have been inspired by this piece from Bihar.

ELEVEN

SHRI SHALKANT VINAYAK

Shri Shalkant Vinayak (11-2), one of the four Vinayaks mentioned in the Manava Grihya Sutras and Yajnavalkya Smriti, is located at the Marwari Kund in Manduadih. This place is situated to the northeast of Bhimchandi Ganesh and is considered the protector of this holy site.

The lower part of the idol is covered with clothes, and it is presented in a seated posture. The features of the crown and the design of the head suggest that it is not from before the sixteenth century, yet other characteristics suggest it might even be from a later time. Thus, the idol has been dated to the eighteenth or nineteenth century.

The trunk of the Shalkant Vinayak idol is turned to the left and touches the bowl of modak held in the upper left hand, indicating its special and worshipful form. The eyes are made like two birds, and the ears are distinctly presented. This unique design sets this idol apart from modern replicas, highlighting its uniqueness and importance.

TWELVE

SHRI KUSHMANDA VINAYAK

Shri Kushmanda Vinayak (12-2) whose name also appears in the Manava Grihya Sutras and Yajnavalkya Smriti, is located in the village of Phulwaria, to the west of Varanasi, amidst mustard fields. This Vinayak is worshiped for removing great accidents and crises, as mentioned in the Kashi Khand, Tristhalisetu, Tirthaprakash, and Merutantra.

Near the temple, an ancient panel of the Sapta Matrikas and a damaged statue of Durga in the form of Mahishasuramardini have been found, further affirming the antiquity of this Vinayak.

The features of the idol are destroyed, and its head is open, which might have had a slight elevation that could have been a headband. The trunk is turned to the left, and Vinayak is in a seated pose, holding a bowl of sweets in the left hand.

Given the presence of the Durga statue and Sapta Matrika panel, and the clear ancientness of the idol, Kushmanda Vinayak can be considered to date back to the eighth or seventh century. It is suggested that the direction and location of Vinayak were specifically chosen based on directional significance, reflecting its religious and spiritual importance.

THIRTEEN

SHRI MUND VINAYAK

Mund Vinayak (13-2), whose idol is located in the wall of the Chandika Devi temple in Sadar Bazaar, is a unique Vinayak. According to the Kashi Khand, this Vinayak's body is in Patal (the netherworld), and its head is in Kashi, worshipped as Mund Vinayak. This Vinayak is located southeast of a Ganapati named Uddanda and is extremely famous. The idol, which represents the head of Vinayak, with large ears and a trunk, imparts a sense of reality. Its features and location certify it as a significant Vinayak.

FOURTEEN
SHRI VIKATDVIJA VINAYAK

Vikatdvija Vinayak (14-2), also known as 'Vinayak with the large trunk', is located in the Dhoopchandi Devi temple in the Dhoopchandi neighborhood. Worshipping this Vinayak is believed to make one the lord of Ganas. Descriptions of this Vinayak are found in the Kashi Khand, Tristhalisetu, Tirthprakash, and Merutantra. The idol is approximately 30 centimeters tall, damaged, and covered in vermilion. The trunk is curved to the left, and it is presented with four hands. However, its hands are damaged, and its features are not clear. Older publications have compared it to a Vinayak from the 5th century, but it is likely an idol from the 10th century.

FIFTEEN

SHRI RAJPUTRA VINAYAK

Rajputra Vinayak (15-2), one of the three Vinayaks mentioned in the Manava Grihya Sutras and Yajnavalkya Smriti, is located near the Rajghat Fort, close to the Adi Keshav Temple. It is worshipped for blessings to regain a lost empire, symbolizing the power of Kashi's rulers. This Vinayak is also mentioned in Tristhalisetu, Tirthprakash, and Merutantra. Most parts of the idol are covered with cloth. The idol's height is approximately 60 centimeters, and it appears ancient.

SIXTEEN

SHRI PRANAVA VINAYAK

Pranava Vinayak (16-2), representing the mantra 'Om', is located on the southern wall of the Hiranyagarbheswar Temple at Trilochan Ghat. According to Kashi Khanda, this Vinayak, known as "Ganadhipa Pranav", is situated on the western bank of the Ganges, south of Rajputra Vinayak, and its worship is considered helpful in achieving salvation. Originally located at Gola Ghat, it is listed in Tristhalisetu and Tirthprakash but known as Pravarana Vinayak in Merutantra. The idol, smaller than 30 centimeters, is depicted in Lalitasana, with a crown and artificial eyes. One of its four hands holds an axe, and another holds a lotus flower. Its trunk and hands are damaged, and it appears flat without ornaments. Based on the crown, it can be considered from the 16th or 17th century.

THE THIRD FOLD OF EIGHT VINAYAKAS

SEVENTEEN

SHRI VAKRATUNDA VINAYAK

Vakratunda Vinayak (17-3), also known as Saraswati Vinayak, is located near a Lakshmi statue outside the Kausatti Yogini Temple, on the wall of Rana Mahal. According to Kashi Khanda, this deity destroys great sins and is located on the northern bank of the Ganges, north of Lambodar. It is also mentioned in Tristhalisetu, Tirthprakash, and Merutantra. The idol is 60 centimeters tall, depicted in a Lalitasana posture with a braid on its head, an elephant-like face, small rectangular ears, and holding a modak bowl in its left hand. One of its four hands holds a noose and another a lotus, while one hand rests on its knees and another holds the modak bowl. The style of the idol seems medieval and can be dated in the context of the Kausatti Devi Temple built in 1807 BCE.

EIGHTEEN

SHRI EKDANTA VINAYAK

Ekdanta Vinayak (18-3), located north of Kootdanta Vinayak and believed to protect Kashi from wars and riots, is situated in the Pushpadanteshwar Temple in Bengali Tola. It is mentioned in Tristhalisetu, Tirthprakash, and Merutantra, where it is referred to as Dantura. The idol is about 20 centimeters tall, in a Lalitasana posture, with elephant-like protuberances on its head and a trunk turned to the left holding a modak. Among its four hands, one holds a noose or axe, and another holds a lotus, while another hand holds a bowl of sweets. The surface of the idol has deteriorated, making it difficult to determine its antiquity and original features. Its resemblance can be seen in Ganesha idols found in the Mathura Museum.

NINETEEN

SHRI TRIMUKHA VINAYAK

Trimukha Vinayak (19-3), whose idol is located in the Tripuranteshwar Temple on Sigra Tila, is described with three distinct faces, while the current idol has three elephant faces. In Kashi Khand, it is mentioned as removing the fears of the people of Kashi. It is mentioned in Tristhalisetu and Tirthprakash, and referred to as Trivadanta in Merutantra. The idol is approximately 26 centimeters tall, with three trunks, one in the middle and the other two curving upwards. The idol is seated on a lotus, holding an axe and a lotus in two of its four hands, while the other two hands rest on the knees, one holding a bowl and the other a book. It has two triangular ears and three eyes, with a large third eye above the middle trunk. The sacred thread and other decorations are identifiable despite being faded. The temple's construction year is cited as 1874, suggesting the idol might also date from this period.

TWENTY

Shri Panchasya Vinayak

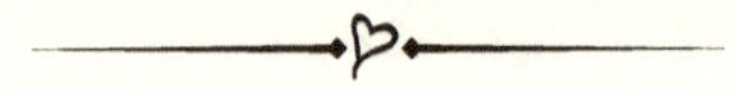

Panchasya Vinayak (20-3), meaning the Five-Faced Vinayak, located in the outer wall of the Pishachmochan Temple in Varanasi, is said to protect the city of Kashi according to Kashi Khand. The idol of this Vinayak is seventy centimeters tall, featuring five trunks, with the central trunk hanging downwards and curved towards the left, while the two outer trunks are shorter. It has four arms, holding a flower, an axe, a rosary, and a book, and is adorned with socks and bracelets. A mouse is depicted at its base, highlighting its uniqueness. The peculiar form of the Five-Faced Vinayak has earned it a place in art books. There are various opinions regarding the era of this idol; it is likely that the idol dates back to the 18th century when the Pishachmochan Temple was constructed.

TWENTY-ONE

SHRI HERAMBA VINAYAK

Heramba Vinayak (21-3), one of the tantric forms of Vinayak, was located in a temple on Valmiki Mound, which collapsed during the monsoon of 1996. Since then, no trace of this temple or idol has been found.

Kashi Khand mentions it as beneficial for the people of Kashi, but does not mention its tantric connections. In the Vidyarnava Tantra and other texts, Heramba is described as having five heads and riding a lion. Descriptions of its idol vary across sources, with some describing it as a Panchamukhi (five-faced) Vinayak and others as Heramba.

An idol located in Vishwanath Gali, believed to be from the 16th to 17th century and associated with a lion, has been identified as Heramba, although there is controversy over the exact era and identification of this idol.

Heramba Vinayak is described in a unique form, depicted as riding a lion, with five heads and ten arms. The main feature of this Vinayak is its lion vehicle, which is also found in the worship of Ganesha in Kashmir, Afghanistan, and Nepal.

The Vidyarnava Tantra lists him among the fourteen forms of Ganesha, and his idol's features are described in various texts. The details of his form and worship practices hold special significance in tantric traditions.

TWENTY-TWO

SHRI VIGHNARAJA VINAYAK

Vighnaraja Vinayak (22-3), known as the 'King who removes obstacles', is located near the Chitrakoot well at J 12/32. According to the Kashi Khanda, it is worshiped for the success of the wise and destroys all obstacles to the south of Vikatadanta. It is also mentioned in the Tristhali Setu, Teerth Prakash, and Meru Tantra. The idol is 88 cm tall, seated in Lalitasana on a lotus seat, with the right leg hanging over a seat. Its ears are small compared to the size of its head, and the trunk is curved to the left. It has four arms, with an axe in the upper right hand, while the lower hands rest on the knees, holding a rosary in the right hand and a book in the left. The idol also features two small elephants.

TWENTY-THREE

Shri Varada Vinayak

Varada Vinayak (23-3), known as the 'Vinayak who grants boons' or 'the fulfiller of desires', is located on the way to Prahlad Ghat. It is specially worshipped for obtaining boons, and it is advised to worship it to the northwest of Rajputra Vinayak. Only half of this Vinayak's idol is visible, highlighting its uniqueness. The height of the idol is approximately 40 cm, and it is likely that it was installed at a new location due to some crisis. The idol shares similarities with the Siddhi Vinayak of Maharashtra, enhancing its significance.

The idol of Varada Vinayak has a large trunk and small ears, and it appears in a Lalitasana posture. It features a modern third eye on its head, indicating its uniqueness. The idol is presumed to have only two arms, suggesting its antiquity. Its current condition and unique form make it special among the Vinayaks of Kashi.

TWENTY-FOUR

SHRI MODAKA PRIYA VINAYAK

Modaka Priya Vinayak (24-3), also known as 'Ganesha Modakapriya', is located at the Adimahadev Temple, A 3/92, behind Trilochan Ghat. This Vinayak is situated on the auspicious bank of the river at Pisangila Tirtha, south of Pranavavighnesha, and is worshipped for obtaining boons. The name of this Vinayak is included in Tristhali Setu, Tirtha Prakasha, and Meru Tantra. The idol's height is forty centimeters, and it is characterized by only showing half of the body.

The idol of Modaka Priya Vinayak does not have a crown, but there is a slight elevation on its head, possibly indicating the presence of a pinnacle initially. The trunk is curved towards the left side, and the carving suggests that it initially touched a modaka (sweet dumpling) vessel. Details of its hands indicate that it was originally depicted with four arms. The features of this idol suggest a dating around the 10th century, making it ancient and significant.

THE FOURTH FOLD OF EIGHT VINAYAKAS

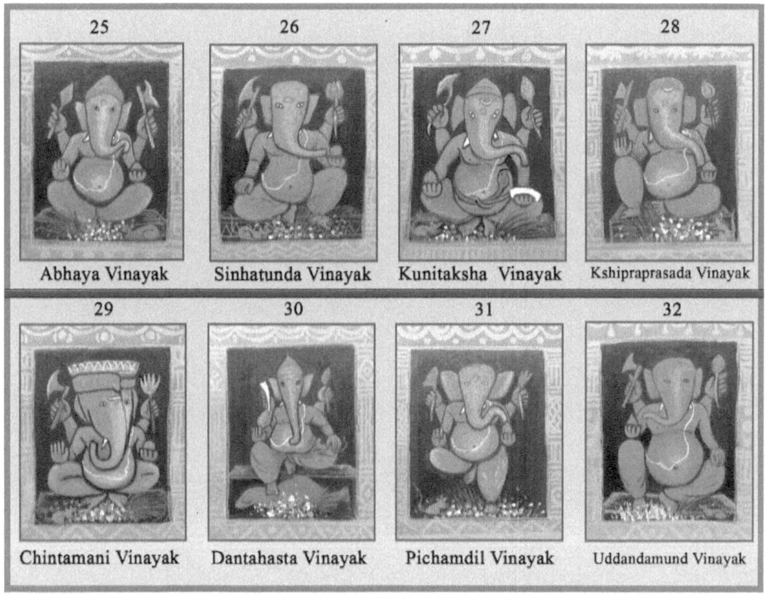

TWENTY-FIVE

SHRI ABHAYA VINAYAK

Abhaya Vinayak (25-4), known as the 'Protector Vinayak', is located at the Shool Tankeshwar Temple on Prayag Ghat. This Vinayak is worshipped to provide a sense of self-protection to those who are frightened, and it is situated north of Vakratunda Vinayak. It is mentioned in Tristhali Setu, Tirtha Prakasha, and Meru Tantra. The idol, about 60 cm high, is seated in the Lalitasana pose with a pinnacle on its head. Its trunk is curved to the left, which is a characteristic feature.

The current condition and damaged state of the idol suggest that it might have been relocated from its original place. It has four arms, but due to damage over time, the objects held in its hands are not identifiable. Based on the four arms and other characteristic features, the idol is dated between the 10th and 12th centuries. The preservation and self-protection attribute of the Abhaya Vinayak idol make it special, and its antiquity and characteristic features afford it a significant place among the Vinayaks of Kashi.

TWENTY-SIX

SHRI SIMHATUNDA VINAYAK

Simhatunda Vinayak (26-4), meaning 'Vinayak with the Nose of a Lion,' is enshrined in the Brahmeshwar Temple located in Khalispura. This Vinayak, positioned north of Ekadanta, is considered a destroyer of obstacles for the residents of Varanasi.

Though its name suggests a 'lion's nose', symbolically, it is regarded for its capability to tackle obstacles. It is also mentioned in Tristhali Setu, Tirtha Prakasha, and Meru Tantra.

The idol stands 40 cm tall in a seated Lalitasana pose. Its head is oddly shaped, indicating it might have originally had a tuft that has since worn away.

The trunk is curved to the left, with carvings that appear to touch a bowl of sweets. It has four hands, with the upper right hand holding a noose and the upper left hand holding a lotus. The lower left hand holds a bowl of sweets, and the lower right hand rests on the knee.

The lower part of the idol is slender and disproportionate, highlighting its antiquity and uniqueness. Determining its exact date is challenging, but based on various features, it could be dated between the 13th and 14th centuries, though some attributes suggest it could be from up to two hundred years later. Its uniqueness and historical significance afford it a special place among Varanasi's Vinayaks.

TWENTY-SEVEN

SHRI KUNITHAKSHA VINAYAK

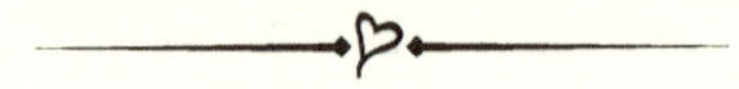

Kunithaksha Vinayak (27-4), known as 'Vinayak with Closed Eyes,' is located at Lakshmi Kund. This Vinayak, positioned northeast of Trimukha Vinayak, is considered a protector of the great cremation grounds. The statue of Kunithaksha Vinayak stands approximately one meter and thirty centimeters tall, depicted in a seated Lalitasana pose.

The statue features an extended serpent sacred thread (Naga Yajnopavita), and its trunk is curved to the left, with two distinct lips visible. It has four hands, one holding a lotus, and another possibly holding either a modak or a pomegranate. The characteristics of this idol present it as one of the fifth-century Vinayak statues, yet its clarity and details suggest a more contemporary period, likely the nineteenth or twentieth century.

The statue of Kunithaksha Vinayak holds a special place among the Vinayaks of Kashi due to its uniqueness and detailed depiction, setting it apart from other Vinayak idols.

TWENTY-EIGHT

SHRI KSHIPRAPRASADA VINAYAK

Kshipraprasada Vinayak (28-4), known as 'Quickly Granting Vinayak,' is located in the Pitaresvara Mahadeva Temple.

This Vinayak protects Varanasi and worshiping him leads to swiftly attained achievements. Kshipraprasada is also mentioned in the Vidyarnava Tantra, where he is described as one of the fourteen forms of Ganesha, with four hands, holding special objects.

However, the pictorial characteristics of his statue located in Varanasi do not match this description. The statue is only thirty centimeters tall and lacks any distinctive jewelry or sacred thread.

The details and craftsmanship set this Vinayak apart from others, and dating it precisely is challenging. Based on stylistic evidence and other features, it is suggested that it could be from the thirteenth or fourteenth century, although a twelfth-century dating is also possible.

The attributes and the capacity to bestow blessings of Kshipraprasada Vinayak grant it a significant place among the Vinayaks of Varanasi.

TWENTY-NINE

SHRI CHINTAMANI VINAYAK

Chintamani Vinayak (29-4), known as the 'Wish-Fulfilling Vinayak,' is located in a small temple on the eastern side of the Ishwarganga Kund in Varanasi. This Vinayak is believed to have the ability to fulfill the desires of its devotees and is considered a wish-fulfilling gem for them. The features of its statue make it special, such as being rootless and the protrusion of the trunk bone, which was quite common around the eighth and ninth centuries.

The height of the Chintamani Vinayak statue is approximately one meter, and its features inform its date. This Vinayak is established in a location that has been inhabited by a Muslim population for centuries, shedding special light on its history. The features and history of this statue give it a significant place among the Vinayaks of Varanasi. Either this statue is not the original Vinayak, or it was hidden during the period of Muslim iconoclasm, which further enhances its historical significance.

THIRTY

SHRI DANTAHASTA VINAYAK

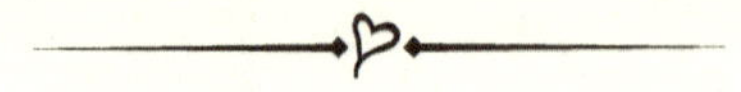

Dantahasta Vinayak (30-4), known as 'Vinayak who Creates Thousands of Obstacles for Those Who Detest Varanasi,' is found within the structure of the large Ganesh temple in Lohatia. This Vinayak's statue is unique because it features a small figure representing a mouse or rat, seated in Vinayak's lap. The statue has large ears on its head, and its trunk hangs down over the body. The statue is about half a meter tall, and its unique characteristic is that Vinayak is holding a pigeon.

Determining the exact period of this statue is challenging, and it appears to be a combination of Lalitasana and a seated posture. Due to several layers of vermilion, most of its features and ornaments are difficult to identify. The uniqueness and characteristics of this statue give it a special place among the Vinayaks of Varanasi, and its dating can be placed in the third period, possibly making it more contemporary.

THIRTY-ONE

SHRI PICHAMDIL VINAYAK

Pichamdil Vinayak (31-4), located southwest of Varada, protects the city surrounded by demons. Its statue stands in a temple at Prahlad Ghat. Its features make it unique, such as standing with bent legs and another small statue wrapped around by a human figure returned by Vinayak, depicting a mouse. Its large ears, crown, and trunk features make it distinguished. This Vinayak is rootless, and the trunk bone protrudes, which was quite common around the eighth and ninth centuries. Pichamdil Vinayak is a blend of styles, and its assistants are referred to as 'Yatudhana,' symbolically representing its protective function. Considering its installation location and time, it is possible that it was hidden during the period of Muslim iconoclasm or its original location was elsewhere. Its features and history provide it with a special place among Varanasi's Vinayaks, dedicated specifically to the city's protection.

ᑭᑭᑭ

THIRTY-TWO

SHRI UDDAND MUND VINAYAK

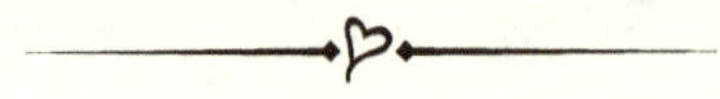

Uddand Mund Vinayak (32-4), also known as 'Vinayak with a stick,' is located behind the Trilochan Temple, near the Trilochan Ghat, behind the Varanasi Devi. According to Kashi Khand, this Vinayak is situated south of Modakpriya on the Pilipila Tirth and blesses its devotees. The statue is not more than 20 centimeters high and is in a significantly damaged condition. The head of the statue appears golden, resembling styles from the 16th to 17th century. The statue is seated, though it's unclear if it's in Lalitasana. The trunk is turned downwards, and the statue has four hands. The dating of this statue is likely post-17th century, evident from its size and the shape of the trunk.

THE FIFTH FOLD OF EIGHT VINAYAKAS

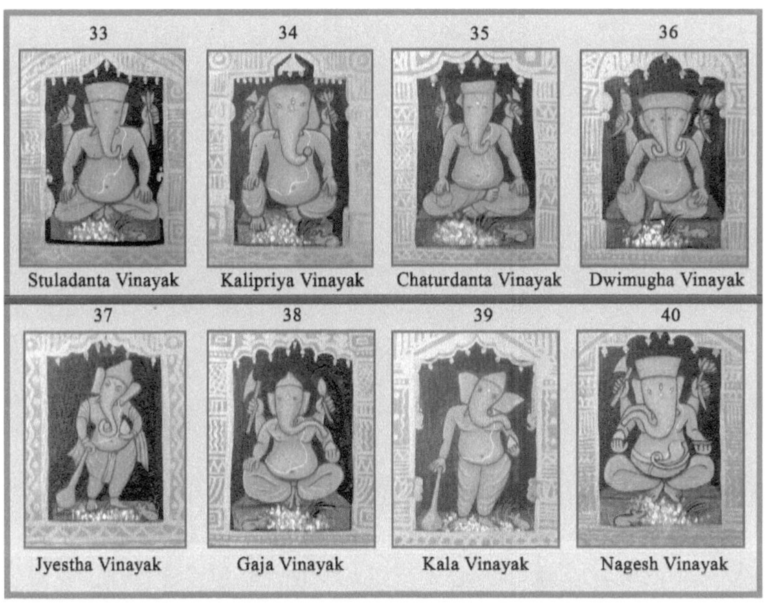

THIRTY-THREE

STHUL DANT VINAYAK

Sthul Dant Vinayak (33-5), whose statue is located in a small temple on Man Mandir Ghat, is described in the Kashi Khand as being situated north of Abhayaprad on the riverbank, providing immense success for good people. However, the current condition of the statue does not match this description and is not suitable for worship, likely due to its deteriorated state. The statue is about 30 centimeters tall, and its most notable feature is its belly, which is half-cut. The trunk and ears are also missing. The statue is seated in Lalitasana, possibly holding a rosary in its right hand. Due to its damaged condition, dating the statue is challenging, but it is likely from the 16th or 17th century, thus it's permanently allocated to the third era.

THIRTY-FOUR

SHRI KALIPRIYA VINAYAK

Kalipriya Vinayak (34-5), located in a small alley in front of Sakshi Vinayak at the Manprakameshwar temple, is mentioned in the Kashi Khand, Tristhali Setu, Tirtha Prakash, and Meru Tantra. Known for causing natural disputes for those who trouble pilgrims, its statue stands about 20 centimeters tall in the Lalitasana pose. Covered in vermilion, its features are not clear, including large ears, a raised forehead, and a trunk turned to the right. It has four arms, with the upper ones holding an axe and a lotus. Another Vinayak statue near the temple entrance is considered by some locals to be the 'real' Kalipriya Vinayak. Its features could date it to the 16th or 17th century. According to Vyasa and Kedarnath, the statue in the temple is part of a group of fifty-six Vinayaks.

THIRTY-FIVE

Shri Chaturdanta Vinayak

Chaturdanta Vinayak (35-5), located outside the temple of Sanatan Dharma School on Nai Sarak, is famous for its unique statue. According to Kashi Khand, it is situated to the northeast of Kunithaksha Vinayak and merely looking at it is said to remove many obstacles. The statue is distinguished by its four arms. It has a crown on its head and its ears are triangular and small. Chaturdanta Vinayak's eyes are closed, and its torso is prominently visible. The lower hands rest on the knees in a meditative pose, suggesting holding a rosary. However, due to the hardness of its surface, identifying its other ornaments is difficult. An indistinct silhouette of a mouse can be identified at the base of the statue. This Vinayak is also mentioned in various ancient texts, adding to its significance. Due to its characteristics and uniqueness, this statue is classified in the third period.

THIRTY-SIX

SHRI DWIMUKHA VINAYAK

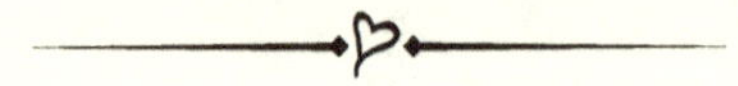

Dwimukha Vinayak's (36-5) statue is installed in the wall of a temple near Surya Kund. This Vinayak, featuring two faces, is not taller than forty centimeters and is in a damaged state. The two faces are not clear, but the presence of elephant tusks on both sides indicates its dual-faced nature. The statue is adorned with a crown and is seated in padmasana (lotus position), with three of its four hands being visible and appearing to be in a meditative posture. This Vinayak statue is considered to be from around the sixth or seventeenth century, marking it as a Vinayak of historical and religious significance.

THIRTY-SEVEN

SHRI JYESHTHA VINAYAK

Jyeshtha Vinayak (37-5), known as the 'Eldest' and 'Greatest,' is located in the Jyeshtheswar temple in Kashipur. The statue wears a cap-like crown, stands in a tribhanga (three-bend) posture, and has its trunk turned to the right. This statue has only two arms, one of which holds a modak. It is forty centimeters tall and is painted in bright colors, giving it a modern appearance. However, its tribhanga posture, two arms, and base on a pedestal present it as an ancient statue. Based on a similar statue in the Dhubeela Museum, it is considered to be from around the tenth century. Its antiquity has been confirmed by various scholars.

THIRTY-EIGHT

SHRI GAJ VINAYAK

Gaj Vinayak (38-5), known as 'Elephant Vinayak,' is located in the Bharbhuteshwar temple, Raja Darwaza area. According to Kashi Khand, worshipping this Vinayak leads to an increase in elephants. This Vinayak is also mentioned in Tristhali Setu, Tirtha Prakash, and Meru Tantra. The statue is forty-five centimeters tall and is in a damaged state. Its trunk is turned to the left, and it has multiple layers of vermilion paint, giving it a distinct appearance. The ears and eyes of Vinayak highlight the sculptural features. It is unclear whether the upper hand is holding an object like a noose. Dating this Vinayak's statue precisely is challenging, but its features suggest an ancient period, though the lack of plasticity could also place it in a later era. Thus, the Gaj Vinayak statue holds a unique characteristic and is identified as belonging to the third period. Its distinctiveness and damaged condition make it an interesting subject for study and worship, marking its significant place in Varanasi's religious and cultural tradition.

THIRTY-NINE

SHRI KALA VINAYAK

Kala Vinayak (39-5), located under a tree near the steps of Rama Ghat, is a 60 cm tall statue that provides courage to not fear darkness. The importance of this Vinayak is mentioned in the Kashi Khand, according to which it is located south of Pichindil Vinayak. It is suggested that its original location was likely between Prahlad Ghat and Gola Ghat, although it has been relocated to its current position. The statue of Kala Vinayak stands in a tribhanga pose, without a trunk but with an upper topknot. Its head is shaped like an elephant's, with the forehead protruding slightly and the trunk curved to the left. It has two arms, one of which holds a modak in the left hand. Its tusks appear small and angry, and its ears are large and wing-shaped. The statue is believed to date back to around the 9th or 10th century, which was previously considered part of the Kala period. This Vinayak is considered special due to the distinctiveness of its sculpture and its significance in the religious culture of Kashi.

FORTY

Sri Nagesh Vinayak

The statue of Nagesh Vinayak (40-5) is located in the Nageshwar temple on Bhonsla Ghat, about which the Kashi Khand states that the devotee is honored by having a vision of Nagesh Ganesha in the Naga world. Originally, this temple was perhaps located at Nagesh Tirtha, which is now Mehta Ghat. The currently situated temple is a small structure that must have held great significance in the past. The statue is 40 cm tall and features a crown that appears like flower petals, a necklace of pearls around the head, an elephant-like head, and a trunk curved to the right. Its right hand touches a modak in the lower portion, while the upper right hand holds a kulas. The left hand holds a kumudini flower and a modak vessel. There is a naga yagnyopaveet on the belly, and its eyes are wing-shaped. The statue lacks any other ornamentation. The features of this statue date it to the 8th or 9th century, indicating its antiquity and religious significance. The Nagesh Vinayak temple and statue hold an important place in the religious tradition of Kashi, providing devotees with a vision and blessing of the Naga world.

THE SIXTH FOLD OF EIGHT VINAYAKAS

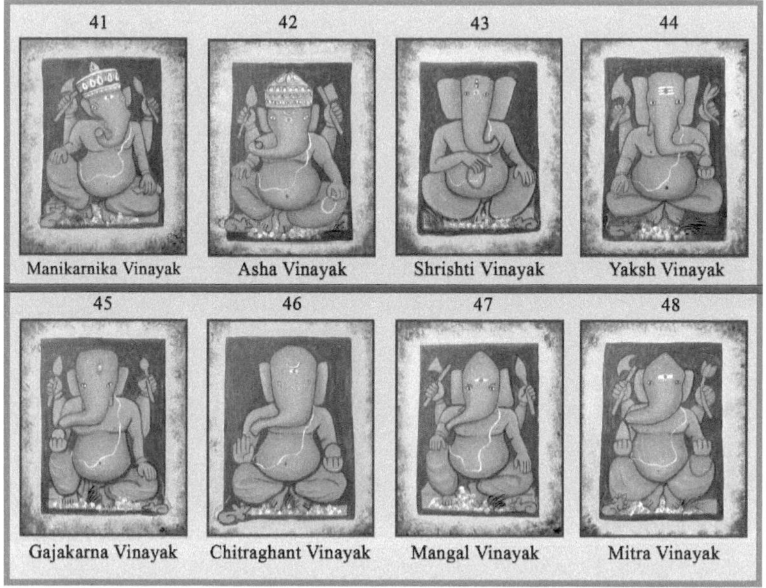

FORTY-ONE

SRI MANIKARNIKA VINAYAK

Manikarnika Vinayak (41-6), named after its location near Manikarnika Ghat, is situated in a nearby temple close to the spot for storing wood for the ghat. According to the Kashi Khand, Manikarnika Vinayak is the destroyer of past obstacles. It is mentioned in the Tristhalisetu and Tirthaprakash, but not included in the Merutantra. The statue is one meter tall and wears a silver crown. The trunk is curved to the right, and it has four arms - the upper right holding a kulang and the upper left holding a lotus flower. One of the lower arms rests on the knee, while the other holds a tal patrika. This Vinayak's statue is seated in lalitasana posture and wears anklets on its feet. Its date is estimated to be before the 18th century, as evidenced by the presence of the masu and the separation of the rear arms.

FORTY-TWO

SRI ASHA VINAYAK

Asha Vinayak (42-6), whose statue is located behind the Hanuman temple at Mir Ghat, is famous for fulfilling the hopes and desires of devotees. The name of this Vinayak reflects this very role. Its statue is about one meter tall and is distinctively depicted in the lalitasana posture. The statue has a golden chandrabindu and possibly a removable silver crown. This Vinayak has four arms - in the upper right is likely a kulang or a decorative lotus flower, while the details of the lower left arm are unclear. The surface has multiple layers of sindoor, making it difficult to identify its features. There are no indications of a yajnopaveet or other ornaments on the statue of Asha Vinayak, but it is adorned with a special dhoti and yajnopaveet on special occasions. Its height and the direction of the curved trunk suggest it is a modern-era statue, meaning it could date from the 9th to the 20th century. Asha Vinayak holds a prominent place in the religious life of Varanasi, and its worship is performed by devotees for the fulfillment of their hopes and desires.

FORTY-THREE

SRI SRISHTI VINAYAK

Sristi Vinayak (43-6), whose small statue is enshrined in a wall in Kalika Gali, is mentioned as a symbol of creation and destruction. Its temple always remains closed, and in 1997, a marble plaque was added below it inscribed with a hymn to Hanuman. Due to this, people often mistake this red-faced figure for Hanuman Bhagwan. The Kashi Khand describes this Vinayak as being located in the south. The statue is 45 centimeters tall, but everything except its face is hidden. Sristi Vinayak has a large third eye on its forehead, and its trunk is curved to the left. Its ears are disproportionately large, and there was one arm on the right side of the body that hung towards the belly, but the other arms or hands are unclear. It is difficult to determine the date of this statue due to its blurred facial features, and no specific era can be attributed to it. Despite the lack of specific information about this Vinayak, it is mentioned in the Kashi Khand, and its physical location and spiritual significance give it an intriguing place in the religious landscape of Varanasi.

FORTY-FOUR

SRI YAKSHA VINAYAK

There are several Yaksha Vinayaks (44-6) in Varanasi, but the specifically mentioned Yaksha Vinayak is located in the Kotwalpur area. This Vinayak is described as the destroyer of all obstacles, and its name appears in various ancient texts. The height of this statue is approximately 28 centimeters, and it exhibits features from the first and second eras. It does not have a cap on its head, and the trunk is curved to the left, touching the sweet held in the lower left hand. The ears are wing-shaped, and the eyes are large. This Vinayak is seated in lalitasana posture, with the lower right hand resting on the knee. The smooth surface of the statue has no yajnopaveet or other ornamentation, indicating its antiquity. This statue represents the transitional skill of its time, and its features make it an important work from the earlier period.

FORTY-FIVE

Sri Gajakarna Vinayak

Gajkarna Vinayak (45-6) - famous by the name 'Vinayak with elephant ears', is located behind the Ishwar Temple in the Kotwalpur area of Varanasi. According to the Kashi Khand, this Vinayak is the cause of welfare for all, and it is also mentioned in ancient texts. The height of this statue is 25 centimeters, and its features make it unique. Its head is like that of an elephant with a trunk and two small tusks. Gajkarna Vinayak stands in a tribhanga pose, holding a flower in the form of a surya parnaka in one hand, while the other hand rests on a bolster. Waves of a dhoti can be seen between its feet, indicating its style as belonging to the early period. This statue has no yajnopaveet or other ornamentation, further enhancing its antiquity. The features and position of Gajkarna Vinayak make it an important work in the religious life of Varanasi, comparable to the temples found around the Lakshmi and Surya Kund. The style and presentation of this statue showcase it as an outstanding work from the early era.

FORTY-SIX

Shri Chitraghanta Vinayak

Chitraghanta Vinayak (46-6) - There is uncertainty about the location of Chitraghanta Vinayak, with two possible sites mentioned by Sukul and Vyas: one near the temple of Chitraghanty Devi in the Rani Kuan area, and another in Chandani Chowk. According to the Kashi Khand, Chitraghanta Vinayak is situated in the north-west of the city, and it is also mentioned in the Tristhalisetu, Tirthaprakash, and Merutantra. The first location is a roadside temple whose door is always closed, and the statue is nothing but a heap of sindoor. The second location is in a shringar temple, where the height of the statue is 40 cm, and it is difficult to see. The head is tall and round, the trunk protrudes outward, and the form of the statue is unclear. The position of the trunk and the indistinct shape place this statue in the modern era. Some believe that this Vinayak is Sthulajangha (Mitra) Vinayak, indicating its antiquity and significance.

FORTY-SEVEN

Shri Mangla Vinayak

Shri Mangla Vinayak (47-6) - The statue of Mangla Vinayak is located in the Mangala Gauri Temple near Bal Ghat, serving to nurture and protect the city in its north-eastern corner. This Vinayak is described in the Kashi Khand, Tristhalisetu, and Tirthaprakash, though it is not mentioned in the Merutantra. In the temple, the statue stands behind the goddess's statue and is not immediately visible upon entry. Due to its positioning, it is difficult to photograph the statue. The Mangala Gauri Temple, known as Mangala Gauri Ghat until the early 20th century, is the oldest temple on Bal Ghat. Its fame and significance date back to medieval times. There is uncertainty regarding the Mangala Vinayak statue as to whether it has always been worshipped as Mangala Vinayak and its location is in the Mangala Gauri Temple or in the Atmaviraishwar Temple. In the Atmaviraishwar Temple, the Vinayak is known as Mitra Vinayak. The Mangala Vinayak statue is around 40 cm tall and is in lalitasana posture. It has a tall crown on its head, and the eyes appear to have been added in modern times. The statue's ears are no longer visible and have likely merged into the background stone. Its trunk is curved to the left and hangs over a large belly. The statue originally had four arms, of which the upper left arm is now missing, and the upper right hand holds an axe. Both lower hands rest on the knees. This statue lacks fluidity or plasticity and does not display any yajnopaveet or ornamentation. Based on its structure and style, this statue could date back to the 16th or 17th century, placing it in the third era.

FORTY-EIGHT

SHRI MITRA VINAYAK

Shri Mitra Vinayak (48-6) - There is a great deal of ambiguity regarding the location and identity of Mitra Vinayak.

In the Kashi Khand, they are mentioned after the eighth Vinayak in the sixth cycle, which brings the total number of Vinayaks to 57. In some modern descriptions, the name Mitra Vinayak appears in place of Sthuljangha Vinayak. Their current location is stated to be near the Atmaviraishwar Temple on Sindhia Ghat, close to the Manikarnika Devi.

According to the Kashi Khand, Mitra Vinayak protects the city of Isha and should be worshipped to the north of Yama Tirtha. Different guidebooks disagree about Mitra Vinayak, with some mentioning them and others not. The location and significance of this Vinayak align with the text of the Kashi Khand, which places them to the north of Yama Tirtha near Manikarnika. The Merutantra mentions this Vinayak, but not the Tristhalisetu and Tirthaprakash, suggesting there may have been confusion between Mitra and Mangala Vinayak in the 16th and 17th centuries.

The statue of Mitra Vinayak is about one meter tall, and its surface appears rough and constructed. The hair on their head is tied, and their eyes are heavy. They are seated in lalitasana posture, and their trunk curves to the right, touching modaks. They have four arms, with a pasha in the upper right hand and a lotus flower in the upper left hand. The lower left hand rests on the knee and holds an akshamala. They wear heavy anklets on their feet and are seated on a structure next to a small rat.

Despite the irregular surface of this statue, it cannot be dated earlier than the 8th century.

THE SEVENTH FOLD OF EIGHT VINAYAKAS

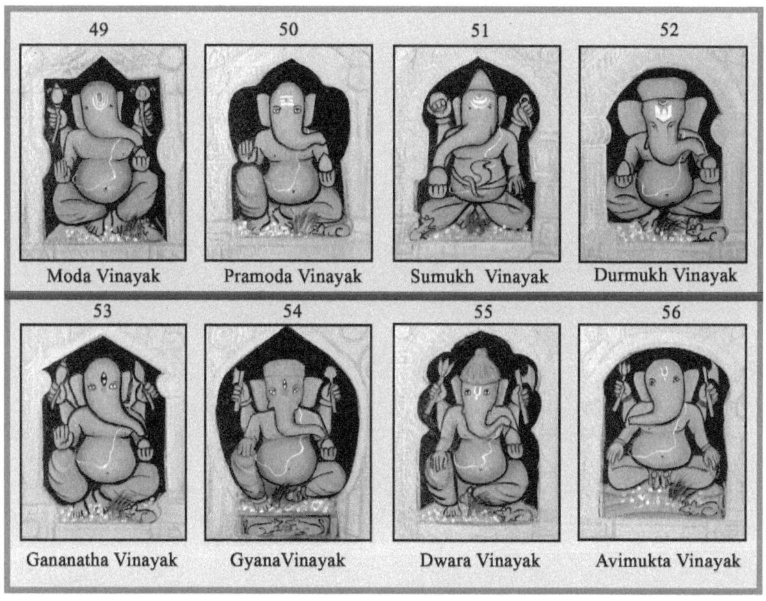

FORTY-NINE

SHRI MOD VINAYAK

Mod Vinayak (49-7), meaning "Vinayak of Joy," is located in the Nepali Khapra temple at the address C.K. 31/12. Photography of this 30 cm tall statue was not permitted, as it is embedded in a wall. Mod Vinayak's features are quite distinctive, such as a crescent moon-shaped carving in a large dot without a bindi on its forehead. There is no longer any trace of ears, suggesting they may have been behind the head and have now merged into the back stone. The trunk curves to the left at nearly a 90-degree angle, indicating it may have been touching a modak vessel. The statue may have originally had four arms, but now only two are visible, and they do not display any attributes. Mod Vinayak's foot position suggests it is in lalitasana posture. There are no indications of ornamentation or a yajnopaveet on the statue. This group of five Vinayaks is known as the Mod Vinayaks, implying that Mod Vinayak is the first and most significant in the group. The features and location of this Vinayak distinguish it from other Vinayaks, and its significance is noted as the deity of joy.

FIFTY

SHRI PRAMOD VINAYAK

Pramod Vinayak (50-7), referred to as the "Vinayak of Utmost Joy," is located in Nepali Khapra, specifically at C.K. 31/16, which is near the location of 'Mod Vinayak.' The features of the statue are unusual, including the absence of a trunk and the presence of three religious symbols on the forehead. Its feet are in lalitasana posture, and the height of the statue is 50 centimeters. It is possible that it originally had four arms, but providing precise details is difficult.

An intriguing aspect of the background and history of this statue is that it may have originally been an image of a Rakshasa or another mythological being, which was accepted as a Vinayak after the Mughal era.

Its unusual posture and the absence of a trunk indicate its distinctive identity. According to the shop owners, the practice of touching this statue was traditionally forbidden, further elevating its significance. Its installation may have been in the context of its proximity to the Vishwanath Temple and its destruction by Aurangzeb, reflecting a tumultuous period in history.

This statue was likely placed in its current position during or after the Mughal era, making its present identity even more mysterious. Its odd form and lack of a trunk suggest that it was originally depicted differently, later becoming acceptable as a Vinayak.

FIFTY-ONE

SHRI SUMUKH VINAYAK

Sumukh Vinayak (51-7), known as the 'Vinayak with a beautiful face', is located near house C.K. 35/7 in Varanasi, roughly opposite Durmukh Vinayak.

This statue is about one meter tall and has an attractive, friendly face. The statue's bulging forehead suggests the presence of a crown. Its trunk and head are somewhat protruding, enhancing its appealing presence. The trunk curves to the left, touching a sweet, and two small tusks are also visible. The statue's ears are large and square.

It appears to have only two arms, not indicating any upper bones on the right. The right hand rests on the knee or holds a round object, possibly a modak or pomegranate. The statue is seated in lalitasana posture, with no indications of a yajnopaveet or other ornamentation, which may be due to its rough surface.

The presence of only two arms could suggest that this statue may be from an ancient era, but due to its lack of fluidity and the specific angle of the curved trunk, it has been placed in the 13th or 14th century. Thus, the statue of Sumukh Vinayak has been assigned to the second era, representing a blend of northern and southern Indian artistic traditions.

It creates a unique identity in the religious and artistic culture of Varanasi, enriching its diverse historical landscape.

FIFTY-TWO

SHRI DURMUKH VINAYAK

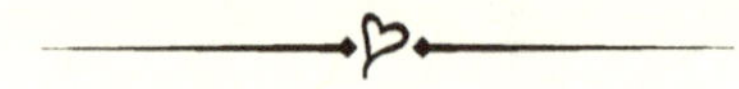

Durmukh Vinayak (52-7), whose statue is located at house number C.K. 35/7 in Varanasi, is about one meter tall. This statue is adorned with a crown in the South Indian style, similar to the conch-shaped crowns seen on the Ganesha statues of Tiruttani and Tirunaraiyur.

Its ears are small and barely visible. The trunk is distinctively broad, curving to the right towards a bowl of sweets. Its right hand holds a round object, which could be a pomegranate or modak. The left hand holds a garland, while its ornamentations are not clear.

A naga yajnopavita is also visible on the belly. Its seated posture is lalitasana, but the feet appear too thin and unrealistic in comparison to the body. The form and style of this statue suggest it is from a recent time, perhaps the 18th century. Its South Indian crown is rare in North India and is associated with the Cola statues of the 9th or 10th century, indicating that this statue was likely created by a South Indian artist who may have come to Varanasi after the decline of the Mughal era.

Its unique appearance can be explained by the fact that the artist may not have had a proper example from South India, resulting in this unique sculpture. Thus, the statue of Durmukh Vinayak makes a unique contribution to the religious and artistic landscape of Varanasi, displaying a blend of South Indian and North Indian artistic traditions.

FIFTY-THREE

SHRI GANANATHA VINAYAK

Gananatha Vinayak (53-7), referred to as the 'leader of the Ganas', is located in Dhundhiraj Gali in Varanasi. The height of its statue is around 30 centimeters, and it is always covered with cloth, making it difficult to obtain details about its complete form.

The statue has a third eye on its forehead, and its trunk curves to the left, indicating that it may have been touching a modak vessel. The pundit has suggested that the Vinayak is installed in lalitasana posture. The features of this statue do not suggest an age earlier than the 17th century. These Vinayaks may be part of the five-Vinayak concept mentioned by Lakshmidhar in the 12th century.

The Kashi Khand has considered them as a unity referred to as the 'five Mod Vinayaks'. However, the Kashi Khand does not provide any details about the geographical location of these Vinayaks. Their proximity to the Vishwanath Temple indicates a lack of clarity regarding their direction. Perhaps, at the time of the composition of the Kashi Khand, they were still present as a group.

Due to the political unrest during the medieval period, there is no similarity in the style or era of these Vinayaks, and they were likely placed in their current locations after the decline of the Mughal Empire. Thus, the existence and location of Ganapati Vinayak present an intriguing puzzle in the religious history of Varanasi, further enriching its diverse historical and cultural landscape.

❧❧❧

FIFTY-FOUR

SHRI GYANA VINAYAK

Gyan Vinayak (54-7), referred to as the 'Vinayak of Knowledge', is located on the southern edge of a large pavilion under which lies the famous Gyan Vapi well. The height of this statue is 1.2 meters, and it depicts three eyes on its forehead.

The statue's face resembles an elephant's head, with a small tusk on one side and no tusk on the other. The trunk curves to the left and touches a bowl of sweets. The left hand of the statue holds a flower that symbolizes the sun, and the right hand holds an axe. The lower right hand rests comfortably on the knee, holding the garland firmly. It wears anklets on its feet and is seated in lalitasana posture.

The statue has a yajnopaveet by its side, and its large ears enhance its beauty. At the base of the statue, there are two mice facing each other. The features and form of this statue suggest that it may have been installed more recently, perhaps in the 20th century.

The Kashi Khand does not mention the geographical evidence of this Vinayak, but its name and location near the Gyan Vapi well indicate its significance. The Kashi Khand extensively describes the glory of the Gyan Vapi well, reinforcing this Vinayak's traditional role associated with knowledge.

This Vinayak not only symbolizes the depths of knowledge but also holds a special place in the religious and cultural landscape of Varanasi.

FIFTY-FIVE

SHRI DWAR VINAYAK

Dwar Vinayak (55-7), also known as the 'Vinayak of the Door', has two potential locations suggested by Sukul and Vyas for its presence. The first location is in the Panch Pandav Temple near the Vishwanath Temple, where the statue is heavily damaged, and only the body remains.

The second location is near the Jawa Vinayak Temple, situated near the Dwar Vinayak Temple while heading towards Manikarnika Ghat. The Kashi Khand describes it as being located 'in front of the Mahadvara', indicating that it was either in front of the temple door or the city gate.

According to Sukul and Vyas, one feature of the Dwar Vinayak statue is its heavy head, which may have been adorned with jata (matted hair) previously. The trunk curves to the left into a modak vessel, and its left hand holds an unknown object. Its upper left hand holds an axe, and the lower hand rests on the knee, perhaps holding an akshamala.

The statue is ekadant (with one tusk) and seated in lalitasana posture. Due to the roughness of the statue's surface, determining its date is difficult, but based on its bodily proportions and features, it is assigned to the second era, the 13th or 14th century.

Despite the lack of clarity regarding the location of this Vinayak, its significance is evident due to the traditional importance associated with its name and location. This Vinayak holds a special place in the religious and cultural landscape of Varanasi, symbolizing protection and preservation at the city's door or in front of the Mahadvara.

FIFTY-SIX

SHRI AVIMUKTA VINAYAK

Shri Avimukta Vinayak (56-7) The statue of Avimukta Vinayak is located to the left of the entrance gate of the Vishwanath Temple, but according to Vyasa, this is a new statue.

The real Avimukta Vinayak is seen in the garbage behind the Knowledge Imparting Mosque. Devotees often worship the revered Avimukta Vinayak at this place.

According to the Kashi Khand, Avimukta Vinayak alleviates all the sufferings of the mind. Despite the damaged condition of the statue, its head and trunk are still visible, indicating a date from the sixteenth or seventeenth century.

Two places have been suggested for the Dwara Vinayak: one near the Vishwanath Temple and the other near the Jav Vinayak Temple. According to the Kashi Khand, it is located in front of the Mahadwara, but its exact location is not clear. The features of this statue and its location date it to the thirteenth or fourteenth century.

Gananath Vinayak, also known as the 'Leader of the Ganas,' is located in Dhoondhiraj Gali. Its statue is always covered with cloth, making it difficult to determine its full details. The condition of the trunk and the possible Lalitasana posture suggest its presence before the seventeenth century.

These statues of Vinayakas illustrate their importance and traditional significance in the religious and cultural landscape of Varanasi, each having its own distinct stories and traditions.

The Locations Of The Fifty-six Vinayakas In Kashi

FIRST FOLD OF EIGHT VINAYAKAS

1 - Ark Vinayak

Near Lolark Kund, opposite to house number 2/17.

2 - Durga Vinayak

At the east corner of Durgakund, in house number 27/1.

3 - Bhimchand Vinayak

In the temple at Panchkroshi Bhimchandi.

4 - Dehli Vinayak

In Panchkroshi Bhatauli village.

5 - Uddanda Vinayak

Near Panchkroshi Rameshwar, in Bhuili village.

6 - Pashapani Vinayak

West of Sadar Bazaar.

7 - Kharva Vinayak

In Rajghat Fort, on Adikeshav Marg.

8 - Siddhi Vinayak

Above the stairs next to Manikarnika Kund, in house number C.K. 9/1.

SECOND FOLD OF EIGHT VINAYAKAS

9 - *Lambodar Vinayak*

Next to Kedar Ghat, on Lalighat.

10 - *Kootdanta Vinayak*

At the site of Kinaram, on Krimikund, in house number B. 3/335.

11 - *Shalkanta Vinayak*

Above Manduadih pond.

12 - *Kushmanda Vinayak*

In Phulwaria village.

13 - *Munda Vinayak*

In Sadar Bazaar, near Chandidevi, close to Chandishwar.

14 - Vikatdvija Vinayak

In Dhoopchandi Muhall, at Dhoopchandi Devi.

15 - Rajputra Vinayak

In Rajghat Fort, beside the road, in house number A. 37/48.

16 - Pranava Vinayak

At Trilochan Ghat Hiranyagarbeshwar.

THIRD FOLD OF EIGHT VINAYAKAS

17 - Vakratunda Vinayaka

Near the well in Lohatia, Bada Ganesh, in house number K. 58/101.

18 - Ekadanta Vinayak

On Pitambara Pura Kedar Marg, house number 7/208, and in Pushpdanteshwar, house number D. 32/102.

19 - Trimukha Vinayak

At Sigra ka Tila, Tripurantakeshwar, house number D. 59/95.

20 - Panchasya Vinayak

At Pishach Mochan, house number C. 21/40.

21 - Heramba Vinayak

Near Pishach Mochan, in Maldahiya Valmiki Tilapar, house number C. 21/14.

22 - Vighnaraja Vinayak

At the pond of Chitrakoot, house number J. 12/32.

23 - Varada Vinayak

On Old Rajghat Road, Prahladghat, house number A. 13/16.

24 - Modakpriya Vinayak

In Trilochan, at the temple of Adimahadev, house number A. 3/92.

FOURTH FOLD OF EIGHT VINAYAKAS

25 - Abhaya Vinayak

At Dashashwamedh, Shooltankeshwar, below ghat, house number D. 17/111.

26 - Sinhatunda Vinayak

In Khalisapura Brahmeshwar, house number 33/66.

27 - Kunitaksha Vinayaka

In Khalisapura Brahmeshwar, house number D. 33/66 and near Lakshmikund, old Lakshmi, house number 52/38.

28 - Kshipraprasada Vinayak

At Pitarkunda, Pitreshwar Mahadev, house number C. 18/47.

29 - Chintamani Vinayak

East of Ishwargangi pond, Babu Bazaar, house number K. 56/42.

30 - Dantahasta Vinayak

Near the well in Lohatia, Bada Ganesh, house number K-58/101.

31 - Pichamdil Vinayak

At Prahlad Ghat, under the Banyan tree, inside the gate, house number A-10/80.

32 - Uddandamund Vinayak

Near the veranda of Trilochan Temple, house number 2/80.

FIFTH FOLD OF EIGHT VINAYAKAS

33 - Sthuladanta Vinayak

At the entrance of Manmandir, Someshwar, house number D-16/34.

34 - Kalipriya Vinayak

On Sakshi Vinayak Marg, at Manahprakameshwar temple, house number D-10/50.

35 - Chaturdanta Vinayak

On New Road, Sanatan Dharma School, house number D 49/10.

36 - Dwimukha Vinayak

West of Suryakund Sambaditya, house number D-51/90.

37 - Jyestha Vinayak

In Kashipura, Jyestheshwar temple, house number K. 62/144.

38 - Gaja Vinayak

At Rajdarwaza, Bharbhuteshwar temple, house number 54/44.

39 - Kala Vinayak

At Ramghat, on the steps, under a tree, house number K 24/10.

40 - Nagesh Vinayak

In Bhonslaghat, Nageshwar temple, house number K. 1/20.

SIXTH FOLD OF EIGHT VINAYAKAS

41 - Manikarnika Vinayak

Next to the wood storage of Vishwanath Singh at Manikarnika.

42 - Asha Vinayak

South of Dharmakup at Meerg

43 - Srishti Vinayak

Outside Kalikagali, house number D. 8/3.

44 - Yaksha Vinayak

In Kotwalpura, Rudraprayag, house number C.K. 37/29.

45 - Gajakarna Vinayak

In Kotwalpura, Ishaneshwar, house number 37/43.

46 - Chitraghanta Vinayak

In Chitraghanta Devi, house number 23/34, and another in Rani Kuan Chandnichowk, house number C.K. 23/25.

47 - Mangal Vinayak

Above Sindhia Ghat, Atmavire

48 - Mitra Vinayak

Above Sindhia Ghat, Atmavire

SEVENTH FOLD OF EIGHT VINAYAKAS

49 - Moda Vinayak

In Nepali Khapra, Kashikarvat, house number C.K. 31/12.

50 - Pramoda Vinayak

In Nepali Khapra, Kashikarvat, house number C.K. 31/16.

51 - Sumukh Vinayak

On the way to Nepali Khapra, Kashikarvat, house number C.K. 34/60.

52 - Durmukh Vinayak

On the way to Nepali Khapra, Kashikarvat, house number C.K. 35/7.

53 - Gananatha Vinayak

In Dhundh Raj Gali, house number C.K. 37/1.

54 - Gyana Vinayak

Next to the Gyanvapi well.

55 - Dwara Vinayak

Near Swargdwareshwar, on Jauvinayak stairs.

56 - Avimukta Vinayak

The ancient idol is missing, laid behind the wall of the deserted Gyanvapi Mosque.

References And Citations

This book has been created by referencing various books like Skanda Purana, various websites on the internet, including Wikipedia, in order to gather valuable information and data. In addition to online sources, this book also draws upon the author's own research and includes references to relevant books in the library. By combining a variety of sources, this book provides a comprehensive and well-researched account of the subject matter. The author has taken care to ensure that all information presented is accurate and properly cited to give credit to the original sources.

Although every effort has been made to ensure the accuracy and completeness of the information presented in this book, human errors may still occur. If any reader discovers an error or omission in this book, I respectfully welcome their feedback and encourage them to bring it to my attention. Such feedback is valuable to me, and I will take all necessary steps to correct any errors and improve the content of this book in future editions. Thank you for your understanding and support.

Contact

Santosh Kumar Singh

9415358375

santoshsinghindiag20@gmail.com

|| LOKAHA SAMASTHAHA SUKHINO BHAVANTU ||

www.ingramcontent.com/pod-product-compliance
Lightning Source LLC
LaVergne TN
LVHW091101150826
845673LV00002B/671

* 9 7 9 8 8 9 2 7 7 5 1 8 2 *